The Principle

of

Success

Lifetime Fundamentals

By Michael Carroll, Jr.

Success is a journey, not a destination – Ben Sweetland

He who gets wisdom loves his own soul; he who cherishes understanding prospers Proverbs 19:8 (NIV)

Published by
Carroll Partners, LLC
4 Daniels Farm Rd
Suite 320
Trumbull, CT 06611

ISBN-10: 0985364009
ISBN-13: 978-0-9853640-0-7

----

*The program developed on these pages is the
direct result of the leadership, guidance and
inspiration of the Father, Son and Holy Spirit to
bring freedom to all people, regardless of
spiritual beliefs, from the burdens of society.
Only when one is truly free can they
experience real success.*

We learn to walk by the time we are one; we learn to ride a bike by the time we're six, about the same time we are starting school. We learn to drive by the time we are sixteen. We get married, have kids and then retire. We do this, most of us anyway, without learning about success. I'm talking about real success. Some of us may have learned society's version of success and that is precisely why we are unhappy and unfulfilled. Of true success, we know very little or even nothing. Many of us never learn what success is and what it isn't. We don't understand what failure is or what it isn't.

If you look around at the world today you will see many people leading unfulfilled, unhappy and unproductive lives. No one ever taught us about success. There are no high school courses on the subject and I have yet to see a college course that teaches life-long principles that, if lived by, will set your destiny in a new trajectory. Well, that's what this program is about. By going through this program and learning to practice this principle alongside the other Principles, you will begin to uncover the life that was meant for *you*. You will realize your uniqueness and finally realize that we are not living in a one-size-fits-all world. You will uncover true happiness as you begin to realize success.

As we begin our journey, I would like to share with you my personal experiences with *success* as the world and popular society defines it and what I have come to know as true, lasting and <u>real</u> success. My journey began, like everyone else, as a child. It's when we are young and impressionable that our beliefs, attitudes and behaviors are formed. They affect the rest of our lives, and for many people, it is never realized that they may develop these characteristics in an atmosphere that isn't or wasn't supportive of real success.

My first experiences with worldly success revolved around sports and money. These two areas were given major emphasis. As I remember I was strongly persuaded to practice baseball everyday and I also had a paper route. I remember hearing from people who had an influence on my life that I could do anything and have as much money as I wanted. Wow, what's wrong with that? So the race was on. Like many young people, my ambitions began to revolve around power, importance, prestige and money. The cues from society, in general, were the same. I should want "stuff" and I should do whatever it takes to get that "stuff." That was *success*!

I took a job as an insurance and investment broker out of college, after seeing the movie "Wall Street." I felt important and there was some feeling of power. After all, I was helping people with their money. There was some feeling of prestige, especially among friends and people who didn't know the industry that well. I didn't make much money though and found out later why. It was not what I was supposed to do. In an industry where they hire almost anybody who walks through the door, I wasn't making the money I thought I deserved. I came to realize years later, that I wasn't working nearly as intelligently or efficiently as I needed to in order to make that money. I would work twelve to sixteen hours a day; I realize now that I was sitting at a desk for twelve to sixteen hours a day, but not really working.

When I met my wife, I remember telling her with an absolute degree of certainty that I was going to be the richest man in the world; I was going to be successful. I don't know if she bought into that or not, but she married me anyway. I think that I might have convinced her somewhere along the way, if she wasn't already convinced. So off we went chasing *success*. After some time of this we figured out what we thought the real problem was, it was the insurance and investment industry. So, I quit my job and took other sales jobs, working equally tiring hours; driving both of us insane with no time for fun or leisure.

I don't think it was until our son came along in 2004 that we realized what we were doing to ourselves. We were working and expending energy toward goals and ideals that were not our own. So what did we do? We quit our jobs. We would be successful on our own, without the help of anyone else. We went and bought some computers, desks, chairs and a two-line phone and went into business for ourselves. Doing what? Well, selling insurance and investments of course. Needless to say, we were not "successful," but we kept up the chase. I don't think it was until we had our daughter in 2007 that we realized what we were doing.

Now I have always been happy with my wife, she is my best friend and business partner. I have the two best kids anyone could have asked or hoped for but I couldn't figure out why I couldn't make any money. Why I couldn't be "successful." I could run 4 miles and work out everyday. I could eat fairly good food; have energy and health. I could have great relationships with my wife and kids, but I couldn't be "successful". As could be anticipated, I was very frustrated. Then, through a series of financial disasters and failures, our eyes began to open. We were *successful*. This program will help to show you how we did it.

We began to realize that we were chasing the world's concept of *success*. We were told what the world thought success was and we pursued it, not realizing that we didn't want it. Being in charge of the world's money supply wasn't in the cards for us. Thank God!

I never realized that I was successful and that I had been for a very long time. I was chasing an idea of success that wasn't mine. Yes, I owned it by the ideas, beliefs and attitudes that I had learned in my childhood and was reinforced in my teenage and early adult years, but I continued to own it for much of my life just because I was not aware of the truth.

When I began to look around, I saw that I had a strong relationship with my Creator. I had the love, friendship and trust of my wife. I had the respect and love of my kids. I had my health and intelligence. I had so many positives in my life, even in spite of the difficulties but I was deceived into thinking that I wasn't worth very much. I now know that I am successful not only because I have all of the things that were mentioned above, but also because of the value and worth I bring to others lives. I don't mean monetary value but the positive comment in the midst of a negative atmosphere. They are the words of encouragement to someone who is feeling down or left out. It's having the conviction to stand my ground on what I believe to be true or right no matter what the consequences. Maybe yes, I have been successful for most of my life.

It's time for you to take a look at your own life. Who defines whether you are successful or not? We all are social creations. We all strive at some level to be accepted. That feeling of acceptance is what many people seek as their measure of success. If people around us are praising us then we must be doing well! So at this point we need to be honest (honesty is a key to success in this program) with ourselves. Friends, family, co-workers or business partners and the expectations of society have determined success in general for most people. It's hard to admit, but it's true, if you examine the things you have been striving for, you are sure to find many of the people who fall into the groups mentioned above have shaped you and your definition of success. But who should define success in your life?

I am going to go out on a limb here; I am suggesting that success should be defined by God and by your relationship with Him. I know that I turned some people off with that statement but I ask you to remember, back in the introduction, where I asked you to suspend all fear, doubt and disbelief. Did you mean it? Are you willing to continue with the program? If what I have to say isn't true, real and relevant to you by the time you complete this program then you can disregard what I say and just go back to your old ways.

Yes, your definition of success should be based on God! It has been said "He who pursues righteousness and love finds life, prosperity and honor."[1] In other words, if you are doing the right things for the right reasons, you *will* be successful.

We are taught at an early age that if we try hard enough we can be whatever we want. I do believe this, to a certain extent, but it misses the point of real success. Yes, if I spend my life working 14 hours a day, 7 days a week staying on top of all the financial journals and magazines, neglecting my wife and kids, forgoing real opportunities to do good in society and to help others then there is a very real possibility that I can be a successful insurance and investment broker. I can make a ton of money, but I would be miserable and so would everyone around me. I would add no real value to the world. I would just be a slave to what I think success is.

Take the example of someone who, without a God given athletic ability, sets out to play basketball in the NBA. He has been told that he can be anything he wants if he sets his mind to it. So he goes out in pursuit of his "dream." He spends his day practicing, giving up opportunities to meet new people, and add value to other people's lives. He may even make it into professional basketball but because that isn't what he was meant to do, there is a tremendous amount of unhappiness. He feels unfulfilled and begins to spend his money on frivolous things. To fill the void in his life he begins experimenting with drugs. He ends up bankrupt and in a rehab somewhere wondering how it happened. Sound extreme? I don't think so! This story is being played out everyday in every sport, in Hollywood and in every other industry. The same thing happens to us even though we are not in the public spotlight. When we give everything we have and push for something we aren't supposed to do we end up bankrupt: spiritually, emotionally, socially and financially.

By allowing your relationship with God to form the basis of your pursuits and aspirations, you are tapping into a source of unlimited power and potential. Yes, YOU WERE CREATED FOR SOMETHING! By pursuing the reasons for your existence you will be more successful than you ever dreamed possible. Success should flow in your life, not be a constant struggle. Yes, there are setbacks and difficult times along the way, but the overall direction of your life and pursuits will all make sense and fall into a pattern of actions, which despite all of the circumstances around you, will move you forward in pursuit of that childhood dream or vision that you had for your life before it was distorted by worldly thinking and influence.

I am not saying that you will have a "free ride" and that your life will be effortless when you find your true purpose and begin to fulfill it, but I will tell you that you will have a sense of peace, serenity and confidence in the face of calamity. You will develop a sense of faith to see you through the hard times and a sense of humility to see you through the easy times.

You will learn to take the next right action in your life and you will begin to see how these tiny actions in your life string together to create success in *every* area of your life.

The victory has already been won. All you need to do is look at the choices you are presented with and make the right ones. Choices as small as holding the door open for the person behind you at the mall or making a phone call in the next 5 minutes to speak to someone who you have been putting off. It doesn't matter what "compartment" the next right action is in, take it in the moment and God will lead you along the path of success. You will enjoy peace and prosperity like never before. Will you give it a try?

Destroy Your Profit Motive

It has been said, "Do not wear yourself out to get rich; have the wisdom to show restraint."[2] I think this truth has been lost in the world today. People run around trying to accumulate things. They work long hours in an effort to get more stuff. They sacrifice time spent with family and friends to feel *successful*. What is the fruit of all this materialism? Everywhere marriages are falling apart; children who never get the benefit of a relationship with their parents, and emptiness and despair as people reach for more of everything.

If your only motivation for trying this program is to make more money and accumulate more stuff, you need to make some hard choices. Is that what you *really* want? Is something telling you that there is more than what you are currently seeking? Will more money and stuff really make you happy? You already know the answers to these questions.

The irony to all of this is, that once you stop the full-on pursuit of money and material possessions, once you begin to practice the rest of the principles in this program, and once you move money down to the bottom of your list of priorities, you will begin to experience *true* wealth, abundance and success. It is here that money will begin to flow into your life. Yes, you will have to put in an honest effort and a fair days work, but that's all you need to do. The rest just happens.

Also, learn to do things without the thought of getting anything back. Volunteer your time, energy and talents to make the lives of everyone you know better. By doing this, you are teaching your brain that there is more than enough time, energy and talents to go around. Your faith will grow and you will know that you have abundance in all areas of your life. I am reminded of an experience Danielle and I had years ago, in 2002. We were sitting outside of a KB Toy Store about four weeks before Christmas. I remember it was snowing and cold. This particular year we had a very hard time financially. I had lost my job over the summer and had not been able to find any work. We had recently bought our house and gotten married. We were discussing whether we were going to go in the toy store to do our yearly shopping for Toys-for-Tots. We had donated to this organization every year since we had known each other. This year was different though; we only had half of our household income coming in each month. We were falling short on our bills and were using our savings to cover the difference. We were both nervous about the finances, but our hearts told us to give. How would we do it since we had no extra money? I'll tell you what we did. We drained our savings account and used that money for the toys. Want to know something? We were okay. We were better than okay. God made sure of it. That following January is when Carroll Partners, LLC was founded (The parent company to Family Coaching Central). In spite of the struggles since the night of that all-important decision, God has ALWAYS taken care of us in our abundance. To be honest with you, there have been *many* times when we have come right down to the moment when we needed Him and He has yet to let us down. So we keep right on going. We give of our time, talents, energy and money without the thought of getting anything back.

In Order to Experience Real Success, You Must First Be A Big Failure

I know many people will scoff at the above words, but they are true. The kind of real success that I am talking about in this program is much more than society's version of success, i.e. a big house, a fancy car and a wad of money. Funny thing is that I happen to know people like that, we all do. Many times those people are not successful because there is no sense of fulfillment and not much to life beyond their career and quest for money. There is the crowd who went to college, got a good job and has been climbing the corporate ladder, never looking back. I am really happy for those types, if they want me to be, but I'm appealing to someone else here.

I am talking to the man or woman who has failed and failed big! Maybe you took a chance on business and lost, you lost all financial security and many possessions. I am talking to the one who may have had relationships shattered or dreams fail. The one who has experienced overwhelming heartbreak and pain. You may have allowed your health to deteriorate to the point where you don't think you can recover. There are an *infinite* number of possible places you have failed in your life. Some of us have had that experience in more than one area of our life. Maybe your whole life has been one miserable failure after another.

Maybe you have lost heart; you can't find the courage, strength, energy or faith to continue. You may feel that you have hit a dead end in life. This, you believe, is how you will finish up your miserable existence. I have good news for you, if you will listen. You are in a great place. You have a chance to experience success on a level you didn't even think was possible. The reason? You can appreciate it. You know where you've been so the success you gain by following this and the other principles in the program will allow you to let that appreciation shine through in everything you do. You will appreciate when things are going well and you will appreciate the challenges, troubles and hardships that lead to personal, emotional and spiritual growth. You will understand the words: "I know what it is to be in need, and I know what it is to have plenty. I have learned the secret of being content in any and every situation, whether well fed or hungry, whether living in plenty or in want."[3] When you have failed you have taken the first step towards success.

The One Who Failed Most of the Time

People who succeed know one important fact; In order to get to success, they must experience failure on a massive scale. For anyone who has read self-help or motivational books, I will not go through the pains of boring you about the countless Hall of Fame baseball players who have failed over 75% of the time (and these guys are the best at what they do). You are probably not a professional baseball player, nor is it likely that you are trying to secure a spot for yourself in the Hall of Fame (if you are, keep reading, this program can help you too). The point is, that the best of the best know this "secret."

Is it possible to live up to your potential and experience real success without failure? I haven't met anyone yet who has done this. There are people living in their comfort zones and are not experiencing failure, but these people are selling themselves short. It's only when you're out there, taking chances and testing your limits, that you will learn valuable lessons and experience the spiritual growth necessary for real success.

The pain of failure causes you to look inward rather than outward. This usually occurs when the pain of failure has become more unbearable than the pain of growing. Sounds painful, huh? It's not that bad when you learn to recognize that the pain of growing will lead you to better things. You begin to embrace that pain and you often begin to seek it out because it leads to a better life. Besides, once you do begin the journey into real success and begin to experience it, the joy, peace, serenity, fun and feelings of accomplishment far outweigh any pain you may experience. It's only when you decide to stand still in life and feel sorry for yourself that the pain becomes excruciating. Take the lessons that you have learned in life and apply them to *your* situation. I don't know what they are for you, but I know that you have them. I read a book recently and I would recommend it to everyone. The name of the book is "Think and Grow Rich," by Napoleon Hill. In this book the author talks about "the seed of an equivalent benefit." Use your failures and pains to grow. It is about finding the lesson to be learned in *every* circumstance and every situation. Even when Thomas Edison was trying to create the light bulb, he failed many times. When asked about these failures, he replied, "I have not failed. I've just found 10,000 ways that won't work."

The good news now, is that you can improve, grow and begin to experience real success without always experiencing pain. If you take this advice and apply it in your life, then your eyes have been opened. You are no longer living in ignorance about your own state of affairs. If you have let your exercise program slip over the last several years you can begin again, today, before the doctor tells you that you need to. If you have been neglecting family or friends because of hectic work schedules, you can leave early today to spend some extra time with those you love, before your kids are grown and the opportunity is lost. If you have been neglecting taking time for yourself, take a quiet walk in the park before the stress of everyday life forces an ailment on you that makes you take a sick day. The point is to do something you want to before you have to do something you don't want to.

See Action Step #1

What Success Isn't: The First Point in Understanding Success

Before defining what real success is for our purpose in this program and hopefully for you as you move forward, it is important to discover what success is not. The world and our troubled society have had a lot to do with most people's current definition of success. If you were to take a field trip to your local mall and stand at one of the entrances, you would get a fair cross section of society. If you asked each person who walked by you to *define* success in their life, you would get many different answers. The answers would be just as varied as the people who pass by. I would be willing to bet, though, that the vast majority of these answers would revolve around the following themes: power, prestige, fame and the big ones, money and possessions.

None of these things bring success in one's life. The first three have nothing to do with real success and probably do a lot more to destroy someone, rather than build them up into who they need to become in order to achieve this elusive animal called success. The other two, money and possessions, definitely play a *part* in the overall picture of one's success, but it is just a *part*.

Let's settle this here and now! Yes, it is okay and even good to have money and possessions in your life. For most people though, it is the other way around, the money and things have them.

Let's look at the typical day for the average person and see where we, as a society, have lost focus on real success. We will use a guy I know. His name is Joe Average. He gets up around 6:30 am with the alarm going off and he probably hits the snooze bar several times; it's about 7:00 am when he finally gets up. He then realizes that he probably shouldn't have stayed up so late last night. He hurries out of the house to start his morning commute to his job that he dislikes or maybe even hates. He knows he should be doing something else with his life, but isn't sure what. He gets to work 5 minutes late and gets right into "making things happen." He is unfocussed and spends ten to twelve hours doing his work. He gets home around 7:00 pm, eats dinner, watches TV, or maybe even meets some friends at the local bar. He then gets to bed late again and starts the whole cycle all over. He does this because he feels he will be "successful" *someday*.

In the meantime, he has neglected the important things in life. He doesn't take care of his health, doesn't do much exercise and probably doesn't eat very well, therefore he lacks energy to have any real passion for living, working and yes, playing. His relationships are superficial, at best. Maybe he is "friends" with some people at work and they go to the bar several nights a week or they play on the company softball team, but the prospect of true friendship just doesn't occur to him. When he does get together with these people it is mostly an attempt to impress each other and to show the others how "together" his life is.

His home life is spent squabbling over such trivial stuff that his home life, where he should have a refuge from the world, has just become an extension of the rest of everything else. If there are kids, there is no real relationship being formed. They all might plop themselves in front of the TV several nights a week but there is no

REAL interaction. As far as plans for the future and accomplishing something greater, well, those dreams died out a long time ago. Rather than living, our friend Joe has settled into a pattern of just existing.

There are so many stories like Mr. Average. The details are different, but the general outcomes are the same. Take Jane Average for example, the other half of the Average family. She does different things, has a different job and different "friends" but the outcome is the same; a feeling of despair and worry about where life is leading. How do I know this? That's where I was for most of my life. Fortunately, I discovered that things could be different, much different, and I have never been so fulfilled in my life. The first move in this direction will occur when you realize that the problem with worldly success is that we were all not created to be rich, powerful and famous. Success is not at some point in the future. It is here and now. The good news is that you can stop chasing the gold at the end of the rainbow; it isn't there. We were all created for a different role and a different experience. This is a good thing and you will begin to see that as you work through this program. In order to move forward, we must first figure out what success is. Start soon though because time is ticking and there are no do-overs.

See Action Step #2

What Success is: The Starting Point

Now that we know what success is not, how do we define what it is? Maybe what you always thought was true has now been turned upside down. That's okay. That's more than okay; you are now at the starting point of an incredible journey. One that may even take you places that you never dreamed you would go. You may even see some old childhood dreams re-emerge. One thing is for sure, if you stay on the path you have now begun, and work at it continually, you will have *real success*. Most of all have fun! Dale Carnegie once said, "People rarely succeed unless they have fun in what they are doing."

Dictionary.com defines success as: the attainment of wealth, position, honors, or the like.

I would like to define success differently. To me, success is constant improvement and movement toward a worthwhile purpose, while constantly raising the bar as you reach small achievements. At the same time, you will be enriching your and everybody else's life that you come in contact with. This definition sounds quite confusing, doesn't it? I can simplify it by saying: *Success is taking the next right action*. Let's take the latter definition rather than the former. They encompass the same thing, but remember I am seeking simplicity and so should you.

You must decide now how you will know when you have achieved success? Because of our worldly programming, most people feel successful by having one or more of the following things occur in their lives:

- Someone tells them they are successful.

- They have an internal feeling of success.

- They measure their achievements.

The first two of these are probably based on our past experience and most likely do not really reveal any success or failure on our part. Rather, they are more of a reflection of us doing what we have been taught by society. The third one can work one of two ways. If you have broken your achievements down sufficiently, then yes, you can use your measurements of achievement to see some success in your life but it does not measure *all* success.

The best way to measure success is to take an honest look at the "fruit" you are producing in your life. Some success if only measured by achievement, can be really discouraging. You may be in a position where you are really working hard to achieve a result in your life. You feel you are getting nowhere. The truth is that you are on the verge of a real breakthrough. Or you may have just been working on a project that may take years to complete. In these situations, it wouldn't be fair to yourself if you were measuring by results. Sometimes the results may be a long way off.

Many years ago I came across a short prayer that I believe encompasses all success. It is called the prayer of St. Francis and here it is:

"Lord, make me an instrument of Your peace.

Where there is hatred, let me sow love;

where there is injury, pardon;

where there is doubt, faith;

where there is despair, hope;

where there is darkness, light;

where there is sadness, joy.

O, Divine Master,

grant that I may not so much seek

to be consoled as to console;

to be understood as to understand;

to be loved as to love;

For it is in giving that we receive;

it is in pardoning that we are pardoned;

it is in dying that we are born again to eternal life. Amen."

I remember when I rediscovered these words several years ago. I was introduced to this prayer as a child, but my mind and spirit were not ready to take hold of the truths that it reveals. Later, as I was doing research for this program, they popped off the computer screen as I was researching success. These words encompass what it means to take the next right action. They will lead to real success in *all* areas of your life.

Let's now examine briefly, the areas in which you should be seeking real success for your life. This list is meant as a guide only; you may add other areas to it, but most of the growth you are seeking in your life will fall under one of these categories. They are in no particular order and will be discussed throughout this program, so I will only list them here.

1. **Vision Success** – Are you doing what you were created to do?

2. **Financial/Material Success** – Figure out how much money you need and then figure out how to get that money.

3. **Family Success** – Your family should be a refuge from the world; a place where you build others up and support those you love most. Is it like that for you?

4. **Relationship Success** – Do you experience fulfilling relationships or are you stressed out with those you spend time with?

5. **Recreational Success** – Life should be fulfilling and fun. Is yours?

6. **Physical/Health Success** – How well you are able to practice this program all depends on how you feel.

7. **Spiritual Success** – The most important aspect for your existence is your relationship with God; it can always be improved.

As you gain real success in these areas, your life will become – satisfying, fulfilling and fun. All of these areas work together to create who you are as a whole person and you need to be focusing on *all* of them in order to make significant progress in *any* of them. For example, you cannot focus only on recreational success without doing any work on your financial matters. This will lead you to poverty. Also, you can't focus only on financial and material gain without working towards improving your relationships. This will lead to lack of fulfillment and loneliness. There are numerous examples and I have known many people who have tried to excel in one or two of these areas without working on them all. Trust me; the result has always been the same. Failure in all areas, even the one or one's they were concentrating on. Take control of your success now by improving your *whole* life.

What is Failure?

Failure is giving up. Failure is taking the lumps and pains that have come your way and crawling in a hole somewhere to feel sorry for yourself. Failure is a way for us to create excuses for not becoming who God wants us to be.

For much of my life I had always thought of failure in a negative way. I thought failure was this horrible monster that was to be avoided at any and all costs. Wow, was I wrong. I have learned that failure, if used properly is actually a stepping stone of success.

What Failure Isn't

As I previously discussed about what success is and is not, I think it is appropriate to have the same discussion about failure, before I move on. If you are to experience *any* success in life, then it is almost certain that you will experience setbacks along the way. In fact, the more success you have, the more "failure" you will encounter before, during and after that success. Remember this and keep it in front of you continually. Print it in big letters and keep it in front of you. Refer to it often.

Setbacks and losses are *not* failures! If you are working towards definite objectives and have a clear vision in your life; if you keep yourself "fit" in all areas of your life then you will have very little to worry about when this "monster," we all call failure, shows up.

By practicing this program, you will be able to move past failure and into a world full of success, filled with possibilities.

A great example of failure is the apostle Paul, before he actually became an apostle. He had everything that was important to the world. He had power, money and what he thought was happiness. Then one day he got knocked off his horse[4]. From there, to keep the story short, I will just tell you that he endured much "failure." The things that he encountered would have made most men or women give up and turn and run into their self made comfort zones. Not Paul, he just kept moving forward, in spite of the pain and setbacks. What he accomplished through all of that is success greater than any man on this earth. For those of you who don't know, Paul wrote the majority of the New Testament in the Bible (The number 1 book seller of all time).

What Permanent Failure Is

It is important to know the difference between permanent failure and temporary failure. Most people never make that distinction. They allow the normal setbacks, that are designed and allowed into our lives to push us along and make us grow, to become life altering and destroying events. They allow these things to sap their energy, and destroy their dreams. They allow bitterness and resentment into their lives.

Dictionary.com defines failure as: a subnormal quantity or quality; an insufficiency. These definitions center around a "lack of success." They are created by a troubled world that does not understand real success and the steps that are needed to create that success. For the purposes of this program and for your purposes, if you really want success in your life, you should understand what real failure is. Failure in life, the real and permanent failure that so many people experience on a regular basis, even as a way of life, is caused by giving up or not even starting in the first place. To make it simple, real failure is sin. You are taking this perfect creation (You) and not fulfilling your potential or destiny. Too many people believe that if they experience loss or setbacks then they are failures. That is the sad state of society today. However, you don't have to live with that belief any longer.

Hopefully you have already begun to ask yourself, "How do I overcome failure then?" Good question! There is a simple answer; *give yourself permission to fail!* One of the guiding beliefs that I have designed my life around is that it is impossible to fail. If I just continue to move forward, even if it's an inch at a time, I will *eventually* reach my destination. It is important to remember, that even if you move forward by an inch, there may be circumstances that put you back 10 feet! Just pick yourself up and start again. It has been said and very appropriately, that *"most of the important things in the world have been accomplished by people who have kept on trying when there seemed to be no hope at all"*[5]. That is true of this program, my life, and if you let it, your life too!

One final note on failure, do not pursue perfection! This is the surest path to a lifetime of frustration and real failure. You cannot achieve perfection! There are probably so many great ideas out there in people's minds, but because they want it to be "perfect" their projects never get off the ground. I am not saying that you should be sloppy or haphazard in your work; just don't wait until everything is perfect before you move forward, otherwise you may be waiting a long time.

The Problem With Traditional "Self-Help" Programs

I remember when I was really young, probably my early teens, I read an ad in a magazine about being able to do or be *anything* I wanted. So, like many other people, I decided to give it a shot. Guess what? It didn't work. I was out about twenty dollars, but even worse, my wallet was open. I pursued these programs, buying new ones as they came out. After all, once a publisher or distributor of "self-help" programs sells you one, you are then on their mailing list and you begin to receive catalogs describing how good things can be, if you only spend a little more money. Like most people, I spent a ton of money, but got nowhere.

"Self-help" programs do not work! They never have and never will. I am sure there's a small percentage of the population who have used these programs and have gotten results, but for most of us, the problem with traditional self-help programs is, you guessed it, they rely on "self." Remember, "self" is what got you into your current mess; "self" most certainly can't get you out. Stop relying on "self."

"Self-help" programs are created by "experts." My experience has been that experts have a way of taking the extremely simple and making it extremely complicated. Sit down with any accountant and discuss taxes with him for just a little while; you will be sorry that you did. Also, step into any gym and watch the personal trainers instructing people on how to exercise. It is the same in virtually *any* field. We humans have a way of doing that.

If a squirrel could talk, and you asked him how he was preparing for winter, he would tell you that he was going to build a nest and store some nuts. Ask a zoologist the same question and you'll get a 300-page textbook. All you need to do to find proof of this in the measurement of human success and happiness, is to look around you at all of the people seeing psychologists and therapists. There are more of these professionals than at any time in human history. At the same time, there are more unhappy people than ever before. They make problems where there are none in an attempt to be important and relevant. In fact, I believe that there are experts in almost every field, including the so called "self-help" experts who, in an attempt to sound intelligent or relevant, will make statements that are so *bizarre* and *outrageous* that others assume they are true. Don't rely on "experts!" I'm not saying you shouldn't take advice from others, you should. Seek people who are getting the results you want and listen to what they are doing. It is clear that you should "listen to advice and accept instructions, and in the end you will be wise."[6]

In other words, don't accept marriage advice from a relationship "expert" who has been divorced 10 times! Traditional "self-help" programs tell you that your success or failure in life, mostly referring to material possessions and money, is up to you and you *alone*. What these programs fail to acknowledge is that your "success" or "failure" is about far more than you - If you only work hard, if you only think positively, if you only fill in the blank. Yes, you need to work hard and think positive thoughts, in fact as Zig Ziglar puts it: "the most practical beautiful, workable philosophy in the world won't work if you won't." Ultimately, your success or failure is far beyond you. Remember, most of the problems in the world are caused by self-reliance. Self-reliance causes your pride and ego to kick into overdrive. Self-reliance causes fear to bubble up to the surface because deep inside of you there is a realization that you aren't capable and need something *bigger* than yourself.

I propose something different. I know it may be difficult, but learn to rely on something bigger than you. I am not saying that it doesn't depend on you at all; I am simply saying that your success or failure depends a lot less on you than you ever thought or were led to believe and a lot more on forces outside of your control. Yes, you need to do the leg-work and supply the willingness, which we will discuss in much more detail later in the program, but for now you just need to stop relying only on yourself!

Most of the traditional "self-help" programs I have seen and tried myself are based on greed and selfishness. You are told that if you follow the prescribed program, at some point in the future a big house, a new car and a suitcase full of money will fall out of the sky, land right in front of you and BAM you'll be happy! They play into our fears and greed. We think these things fill the voids in our lives and they do, temporarily, until we are no longer satisfied and we want more. These programs talk very little of real and lasting success.

Self-help programs just don't work. Yes, you can improve by carefully selecting and implementing a self-help program. What I have found though, is the improvements are usually temporary and most people return to their old behaviors shortly after trying the program. The reason is because most of these programs focus only on the surface stuff. They don't dig deep into a person's character to uncover and fix the character issues that are holding them back from achieving their full potential. If you are trying this program I am sure that this is probably not your first attempt at trying to improve yourself or become "successful." If you follow *this* program and continually work at it, this will be the last program that you will ever need. Give yourself permission to try as you go through this program and you will be amazed at the results. This program works!

It's important to realize that this program is *not "self-help!"* You must admit here and now, that up to the point where you started this program, your self-run life was not really working out the best that it could. You may have been "surviving" or "getting by" but as for real success you have not really seen too much. Without that first admission and initial honesty, you may as well give this program away to someone else.

"Self-help" programs simply do not work for real and lasting results in your life. I said this before, I researched many "self-help" programs and admit that there are many good insights and lessons that can be taken and learned from some of these programs. In this program, I did the research for you. We sorted through the good and the bad, the great and the horribly bad lessons and advice. The information and advice that is worth applying in your life is in *this* program.

Self is what got you into your current circumstances and situations. While they are not all bad, you must first admit and realize what brought you to the starting point of this program. Now is the time to really begin leaning on something bigger than yourself. You will be doing things along the way to make your life better and you more successful, but you are not the cause of any success you may enjoy. It is God! (Remember, that at the start of this program you agreed to suspend your fear, doubt and disbelief?) When you first realize this and then accept it, you will see how you receive guidance and direction, but you take the actual steps. If you *do* believe, then there is no convincing needed. I simply ask that for the duration of this program you place your trust in Him and allow good things to follow.

This program, if followed and acted upon, will have a tremendous impact on your life and for many people, it will introduce them to real success. Before I talk about all of the positives, let's take a moment to discuss what the program will *not* do. There are many people looking for a "quick-fix" for all of life's problems. This program is not that "quick-fix." There is hard work ahead for you if you expect to achieve real success in your life. Yes, it's worth it! You will not lose 300 pounds in the next seven days, nor will you become a billionaire in the next thirty. Your life will not become problem free nor will you make all of your relationships stronger than ever before, when you wake up tomorrow. You will not be an Olympic athlete in the next 6 weeks; you will not move your family into a mansion on the beach in two weeks and buy the yacht you always thought you deserved in three weeks.

So *what* will this program do? It will give you more than you ever dreamed possible. I talk to many people who are not even clear about *what* they want. This program will help you clarify what is really important. Most of the time what you thought you really wanted is nothing in comparison to the plans God has for you and your life. Yes, you *will* gain material objects such as a new house and more money. Your relationships *will* get better; your health *will* improve and the list goes on and on. It's safe to say that every area of your life that is worth improving, will improve. However, it's important to remember that it will take time and patience.

You will have direction and guidance. Your priorities will change and so will your goals and dreams (if they have been misdirected up to this point). I can only tell you from experience, that my life is nothing like I thought it would be, and my life is *better* than I could have ever dreamed possible.

Until creating this program and living by the principles set forth, I had no idea how good things could get. In spite of the difficulties and hardships, things are GOOD! They can be for you too. Are you ready? It has been said that, "whoever accepts guidance and seeks God will be blessed."[7] If you are doubting this statement, just give it a try and you will see that it is true.

The best thing you will gain from this program is "the peace that passes all understanding"[8] You will have peace and serenity in your life *regardless* of what is happening around you. Many programs out there claim that if you only do what they say, you will have no problems or challenges and life will be perfect. If that is what you are aiming for in life, then you don't understand real success. Real success is moving forward, in spite of difficulties. Although you will still have problems and difficulties, even if you work this program perfectly, (which is impossible), I can tell you that your problems, difficulties and challenges will change. As you conquer your present ones, you will grow. As you grow, you will be presented with new problems, difficulties and challenges. Through all of this, if you maintain your focus on this program and your desire to grow, you will maintain peace and serenity in your life. This will spread to everyone around you and you will be a force for positive and good in other people's lives, as well as your own.

Things To Remember While Pursuing Real Success

There are several things I ask you to keep in mind as you are learning to grasp this new concept of success. These tips will help you to *thoroughly* evaluate where you stand with regards to real success in your life. Some of them have been mentioned already and all of them will be mentioned again throughout this program.

The first thing to remember is that "experts" complicate things. This is not to say that you shouldn't seek help or ask for guidance when you need it. I think seeking advice is very important. "Plans are established by seeking advice..."[9] I *am* saying you should ask people who are getting the results you are seeking. Don't ask someone simply because they are an "expert." Also, don't avoid asking someone, simply because they are not formally educated on a topic. I remember when I used to pay hundreds of dollars to have the brakes done on my car. The mechanic would make the procedure sound difficult and complicated. Then one day, without enough money to get a much needed brake job, I decided to do some research. What I found was how amazingly simple doing a brake job is. If you can change a tire you can fix your brakes.[10] I have since saved thousands of dollars because I stopped relying on "the experts."

T.D. Jakes has said: "Success can be as painful as failure if you are not equipped for it." You must be *ready* for it. When success comes, usually after a season of long struggles, it comes fast. Don't allow it to overwhelm you. Make sure that you are prepared. The best way you can do that is to make sure you are constantly practicing all of the fundamentals in this program. You will make mistakes in practicing these principles, but after each mistake be sure that you get up and continue to move forward.

Remember that success and achievement are different. In many cases they do go together and complement each other. They also may be independent of each other in certain circumstances. You may go to the gym everyday to work on your physical health (success) but you haven't set a goal to run a triathlon or a marathon (achievement). As you can see from the above example, they can go together. Obviously if you are training for a marathon you will be healthy but you don't have to run a marathon in order to be successful at improving your health. The Principle of Achievement, part of this program, will be discussed at a later time. Right now it's important for you to focus on real success. Achievement *will* come and you will learn how to figure out what to achieve and just as importantly why to achieve something.

There are certain tools and attitudes you need to be introduced to. These will help you use the program and get maximum benefits in the shortest amount of time. You have probably heard of or used these tools or attitudes at some point in your life. In order to move forward I will mention each only briefly but they will be developed further as I go through the program:

1. **Prayer**: "Pray continually."[11] For now, just pray the best you can. If you can't do that, just talk about the good things in your life in your head.

See Action Step #3

2. **Quiet Time**: You need to learn to be alone with yourself and more importantly, to be at peace with yourself while you are alone. The only way to get good at this is to just do it. Start small, around 5 minutes and gradually add time until you can sit quietly by yourself for at least one hour a day.

See Action Step #4

3. **Visualization**: Visualization is a tool that I have found to be extremely helpful. It is not the *key* to success, like so many programs claim, but it is a useful instrument. It comes more naturally to some people than to others. If you are already good at it, use it. If not, practice until it becomes effortless. You only need to use this for 15 minutes a day. I have found that it works best when you go to sleep 15 minutes earlier than normal and spend that time visualizing the things, behaviors and attitudes you want in your life.

See Action Step #5

4. **Have an Open Mind**: The concepts I will be discussing may seem foreign or awkward at times, but remember that you have spent most of your life learning things that work contrary to success. These are the tools and attitudes that have worked for me and countless others. Remember that you can always go back to your old ways whenever you want; just give this program an honest try first.

See Action Step #6

5. **Persistence**: Be persistent and if that doesn't seem to be working, KEEP BEING PERSISTENT! Stay with this program, it will work! You just have to keep yourself wanting a better life. Avoid comfort zones that tend to keep people down. One good way to stay

with it, when it seems time to quit, is to make a list of all of the stimuli that motivates you or keeps you positive. Think of songs, poems, quotes, etc. Thomas Watson once said, "You can be discouraged by failure or you can learn from it, so go ahead and make mistakes. Make all you can. Because remember that's where you will find success."

See Action Step #7

The Beginning: Real Success

The first thing we need to determine is who you are *now*. This may seem like an easy task at first and it should be easy, but I believe that there has been so much confusion about who or what a person should be, that they might be unable to define who *they* are. The good news is that after being involved with this program for a short time, it will become easier to answer the question: Who are you? Once you are able to answer this question clearly and truthfully, it will be easier for you to determine who you want to become.

I have found that who you are now is based on many different factors; the most important being your beliefs, experiences, decisions and personal expectations. Let's take a look at each one of these individually. We will see in a minute that they are all related.

• **Beliefs:** What you believe has an enormous impact on your actions and therefore who you are. If you believe you are successful, then you are. If you believe you can't be successful, then you never will be.

• **Experiences:** *Every* experience - good, bad or even neutral - plays a significant role in who you have become up to this point in your life.

• **Decisions:** *Every* decision you have ever made has had a direct impact on where you are in your life today, even the small, insignificant ones.

• **Personal Expectations:** You will only go as far as you *expect* to; things can only get as good as you expect. They can also become as bad as you expect.

All of these components of who you are now, have been formed throughout your lifetime by experiences, *both* good and bad. They come from things that have happened to you. They are things that you allowed or things that were against your will. *Everything* that has happened in your life shapes who you are at this moment and as you can see from the diagram below that it is all related:

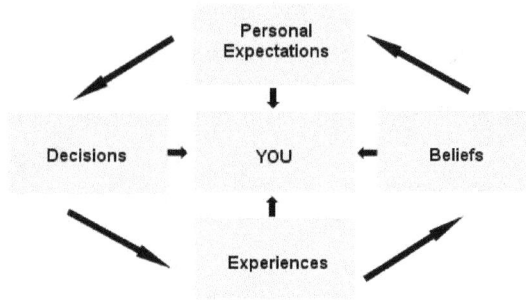

The chart above may at first look very complicated and intimidating, but it is actually quite simple. What I am trying to convey is the fact that who you are today has been influenced by the above components of your life. Once you understand it, it will be good news.

Let's use as an example, somebody's health, and we'll look at it from both positive and negative perspectives. Let's look at the negative first. Suppose as a child, your parents were always expecting you to catch the measles or come down with the latest strain of the flu virus. As a young, impressionable child you tended to believe your parents (personal expectations). Since you "knew" you were going to get sick, you figured why wash your hands or take any other precautions (decisions). What happened? You got sick (experiences)! Over time you began to think that it was only normal to get sick (beliefs). It was only natural that you would begin to expect yourself to continue to be sick (personal expectations, again). We could continue to go around and around this chart, as so many people do in real life, with each step strengthening the expectations, decisions, experiences and beliefs all the way through to adulthood where, today, you have a *constant* struggle to stay healthy.

You may on the other hand, have had a much more positive experience. You may have had parents who taught you that you were meant to be healthy and that your body wasn't meant to get sick (personal expectations). So what did you do? You washed your hands before eating; you ate foods that strengthened your body (decisions). Because of this, you usually were healthy and you began to see the results of your actions (experiences). So you began to expect yourself to stay healthy (beliefs). This in turn strengthened your personal expectations. Like the negative example, we can go around and around the chart to your health today; which I expect is good.

I know this to be true from personal experience, as well as from watching other people. As an adult I rarely get sick and my two children and wife are the same. This is true despite being exposed to the same "hazards" as any other people. I can see it everywhere I go. Those who expect sickness, get sickness. It is the same with every other area of your life. Following this program will help you interrupt this pattern from all four directions. You will change your personal expectations, decisions, experiences and beliefs *simultaneously*.

See Action Step #8

Another important, but difficult, way to find out about yourself is to *simply* ask someone. I know it's hard. I know it may be embarrassing. Do it *anyway*! I am sure that there are many people who will put the program down and never look at it again because of this simple request. Those who get beyond their pride and ego will learn a great deal about themselves. You will find a list of questions to ask in the activities section.

Who should you ask? Some good choices for this activity are those who know you very well. Try to find someone who knows about most aspects of your life. Someone who knows you personally, professionally and recreationally would work best. You should try to find someone who knows about your family situation too. Don't use your spouse, unless your relationship can handle a little honesty and criticism (your second time through this program you should be able to do this, but be careful your first time through). A friend, family member, or possibly someone from your church, may work your first time. Let them take form 1-9 home and *think* about the answers before writing them down. This will give you the best results. After this is completed you will have a "snap shot" of yourself. What do you think?

See Action Step #9

Do you like who you are?

If you do, that's great, but I am sure that there are areas in your life that need changing or improving, otherwise this program wouldn't have interested you.

If you don't like the results of some of the activities up to this point, then you are in the right place. I suspect that most people, who have been honest with themselves up to this point, will fall into the latter.

See Action Step #10

Remember, if you fall into the second category, stick with this program, things *will* improve. Through the course of the program you will learn to change one or more of the aspects of who you are now (beliefs, experiences, decisions and personal expectations). This will in turn cause even *more* positive changes in your life. It is called interrupting your pattern and you will learn to do it just by following through on your activities. For now, let me give you a quick way to interrupt the negative patterns in your life so that you can begin right away. It starts by visualizing the behavior that you don't like or that you want to change. While you have that visualization going on in your mind, create a second scene with the behavior you *do* want. Make the good behavior or scenario come down from the sky, crashing onto and crushing the old undesirable behavior. It sounds complicated, because experts have made it so, but just practice and you you'll get it!

See Action Step #11

Who Do You Want To Be?

It's a great question, but so few people have actually thought much about the answer. It's easy to avoid this topic, especially if you have been caught up in the world's version of success. You have probably been too busy to think this through logically but you can now. Answer this question in **Activity 12** now. Don't just write: I want to be a good person or a better spouse or a better parent. Describe your life in *detail*. Look at every facet of your life. Write about your relationships, finances, health, spirituality and any other area of your life that you would like to change or improve. Why are you doing this? Because you *become* what you think about. The Roman emperor, Marcus Aurelius said, "A man's life is what his thought makes of it."

A person who is constantly thinking about living successfully and has a clear vision of who they want to be and what they want to do will become that vision, because that is what they are focusing on. These people will have peace, serenity, happiness, success and love in their lives. A person who is constantly thinking about living in failure and does not have a clear vision will fail to live successfully. These people will live with constant fear, worry, turmoil, anger and confusion. If you spend your time thinking about nothing, you will become nothing.

See Action Step #12

Conclusion

Going back in human history, something was lost along the way. We, as humans, are no longer living the way we were intended to. We were not supposed to bury ourselves in busyness, hoping that if we just had more money, everything would be great. No, we were *meant* for a life of fulfillment. We each have a purpose and a plan that was created *especially* for us. It is our job to figure out what that purpose and plan is. That is what will fit into our lives; it will give us all of the success we want and need.

As you complete the activities for this first principle you may feel awkward and maybe even a little uncomfortable; that's okay. You are just beginning to awaken the *real* you. The you that has been buried under layers of programming you have been receiving your entire life. That feeling will fade as you get used to living your new life. It will soon be replaced by a feeling of peace, serenity and happiness that you never realized you could experience.

As you change and begin to experience real success, you may encounter resistance. In some cases this resistance may come from the people *closest* to you. Just remember these words, "if you change something and no one gets upset then you just changed something that doesn't matter."[12] You are changing something very important...YOU! The changes are for the better but people you know will get uncomfortable. Just keep moving forward and maybe one day you will be able to help them make the changes they need to make.

<u>Summary</u>

- You are created for a purpose.
- Learn to destroy your profit motive.
- To experience real success, experience failure on a massive scale.
- What success isn't: power, prestige, fame, money and material things (no one of these by themselves brings true success).
- What success is: taking the next right action.
- Achievement does not measure all success.
- Measure success by the fruit you are producing in your life.
- 7 areas of success:
  - Vision
  - Financial/Material
  - Family
  - Relationship
  - Recreational
  - Physical/Health
  - Spiritual
- Setbacks and losses are not failures
- Permanent failure is giving up or not even trying
- Real failure is sin!
- Things to remember while pursuing real success:
  - Experts complicate things.
  - Success and achievement are two different things.
  - 5 Tools and attitudes for success
  - Prayer
  - Quiet Time
  - Visualization
  - Open Mind
  - Persistence
- Determine who you are now by looking at:
  - Beliefs
  - Experiences
  - Decisions
  - Personal Expectations.
- Who do you want to be?

Prayer

Lord Teach me about true and lasting success. Help me to see success in the things I do and in who I am on a daily basis.

Amen.

Action Steps

What they are: They are small steps that you take everyday; to bring you closer to the person you want to be. They are designed to create momentum in following the FCC plan.

Why they are: People are more likely to follow through on taking action, if they don't have to figure out what actions are necessary in order to grow.

Action Step1 ~
Be Proactive

In this Action step you are going to learn how to be proactive about your success. Do something today, proactively, doing it out of pleasure and because you want to before the pain associated with it becomes too great and you are forced to act.

1. What area of your live do you need to work on today?

_____

_____

_____

2. Why have you been procrastinating doing it?

_____

_____

_____

3. What is the one proactive action you will take today toward making the change?

_____

_____

_____

4. Log your success. What are your thoughts, ideas and feelings about being proactive?

_____

_____

_____

Action Step 2 –

Your Life

For this Action Step, I want you to imagine, briefly, that your time was up on this earth and you were given only 1 week to live. How would you answer the following questions?

1. As you reflect on your life, what do you wish you had done more of?

_____

_____

_____

2. What do you wish you had done less of?

_____

_____

_____

3. What does your life represent?

_____

_____

_____

4. What song would you want played at your funeral? Why?

_____

_____

_____

5. If you knew you had 1 week left, what would you do?

_____

_____

_____

Action Step 3 ~

Prayer

In this Action Step you are going to begin using prayer to help you produce success in your life. Begin by just praying about success.

1. Set up a specific time each day when you can pray without getting interrupted. When is it? Put it on your calendar if you need to.

_____

_____

_____

2. What areas of your life do you need to pray about?

_____

_____

_____

3. Log your success. After spending time in prayer...how do you feel?

_____

_____

_____

_____

_____

_____

_____

_____

_____

Action Step 4 –

Quiet Time

For this Action Step, you are going to learn to develop a time where you can be by yourself. Do the following activities. Start by taking 5 minutes of quiet time; gradually increase it by 1 minute per day until you get to 60 minutes.

1. Set up a specific time each day when you can take quiet time without getting interrupted. When is it? Put it on your calendar if you need to.

_____

_____

_____

2. Find a place where you can take quiet time without getting interrupted. Where is it?

_____

_____

_____

3. Log your success. Use this form to write down your thoughts, ideas and feeling from your quiet time.

_____

_____

_____

_____

_____

Action Step 5 –

Visualize

In this Action Step you are going to practice visualizing the success you want. Go to bed 15 minutes earlier than you normally would. Spend this time visualizing the things, behaviors and attitudes you want in your life.

1. Before heading to bed get clear about what you'll be visualizing. Write down the areas that you want to focus on today. Having a clear direction for visualization will make the impact even greater.

_____

_____

_____

_____

_____

_____

_____

_____

2. **Log your success.** Use this form to write down your thoughts, ideas and feelings from your visualization.

_____

_____

_____

_____

_____

_____

Action Step 6 –

Open Mind

In this Action Step you will learn to open your mind. This will help you to overcome false beliefs that you have learned over the years that work contrary to success. With an open mind, pick one aspect of The principle of Real Success that you disagree with or don't want to do and try it.

1. What is the thing(s) mentioned in this principle that you disagree with?

_____

_____

2. What are a few things that you could do to test this for its validity?

_____

_____

_____

3. Now pick one of the items listed above in number 2, and do it. Write down your thoughts, ideas and feelings after trying it out.

_____

_____

_____

4. Have your beliefs changed? Why or why not?

_____

_____

_____

Action Step 7 –

Persistence

In this Action Step you are going to develop a set of tools to help you remain persistent, even when you are experiencing difficulties.

1. Make a list of everything that motivates you. Include songs, quotes, poems, etc. Refer to this list often when you are feeling a lack of motivation.

List of motivations:

_____   _____

_____   _____

_____   _____

_____   _____

_____   _____

2. Think of a time when you followed through during a difficult time. What was it?

_____

_____

3. How did you get yourself to follow through?

_____

_____

_____

4. Log your success. What are your thoughts, ideas and feelings about persistence?

_____

_____

_____

Action Step 8 –

Examine Your Life

In this Action Step you are going to examine your personal expectations, decisions, experience and beliefs that have influenced your life both positively and negatively.

1.   Pick one area of your life that you are experiencing success in.   List your personal expectations, decisions that you have made and your experiences with this area and your beliefs about this area of your life.

a.   The area of my life that is going as I want it to is:

_____

_____

_____

b.   My expectations for this area are:

_____

_____

_____

c.   My decision for this area have been:

_____

_____

_____

d.   My experiences in this area have been:

_____

_____

_____

e. My beliefs about this area are/have been:

_____

_____

_____

2. **Now do the same for 1 area that isn't going so well.**

   a. The area of my life that is not going as I want it to is:

   _____

   _____

   _____

   b. My expectations for this area are (what should they be?):

   _____

   _____

   c. My decision for this area have been (what should they be?):

   _____

   _____

   d. My experiences in this area have been (what should they be?):

   _____

   _____

   e. My beliefs about this area are/have been (what should they be?):

   _____

   _____

Action Step 9 –

Ask Someone

In this Action Step you are going to ask someone about yourself. Ask them the following questions and be prepared if the answers are not what you wanted or expected. Promise the person that they can be honest and you won't get mad or upset...and keep your promise!

This works best if you give them form 9-1 to fill out (on the next page). Let them think about the answers and write them down. Don't put them on the spot!

Form 9-1

Dear _____,

I am in the process of trying to improve my life with the help of Family Coaching Central (www.lifetimefundamentals.com). Part of the process is for me to pick someone I know well to tell me about myself. I picked you. Will you take a few minutes to answer these questions? I promise that I will not get angry or upset with your answers.

1. Do you know what some of the guiding beliefs in my life are?

_____

_____

_____

2. Can you tell me which experiences in my life have impacted me the most?

_____

_____

_____

3. Which of my decisions have had the most impact on my life and why?

_____

_____

_____

4. Describe my personal expectations. Am I hard/easy on myself or do I treat myself fairly?

_____

_____

_____

_____

_____

_____

5. What else should I know about myself from your perspective and experiences?

_____

_____

_____

_____

_____

_____

Action Step 10 –

Do you like you?

In this Action Step you are going to be honest with yourself about *YOU*. Do the following activities:

1. **Are you happy with you?** If Yes, Why?

_____

_____

_____

2. What can be changed to make you even better?

_____

_____

_____

3. If no, what are you unhappy about?

_____

_____

_____

4. Why are you unhappy about this area of your life?

_____

_____

_____

5. What can be changed to make you improve?

_____

_____

_____

6. What are your thoughts, ideas and feelings about yourself?

_____

_____

_____

_____

_____

_____

Action Step 11 –

Interrupting Patterns

In this Action Step you are going to practice interrupting a negative pattern in order to create a new, positive behavior. Interrupt a Pattern. Practice this as often as possible. Do it until you get good at it.

1. What's the pattern/habit you want to end?

_____

_____

_____

2. Why do you want to interrupt this pattern/habit?

_____

_____

_____

3. What action will you take to interrupt the pattern/habit?

_____

_____

_____

4. Interrupt the pattern of your behavior, as outlined on page 27. What are you thought, ideas and feelings?

_____

_____

_____

5. **Log your success:** Every time you know you would have repeated this pattern/habit but didn't fall into the trap, write it down. Seeing your successes makes it easier to continue and you can also see HOW you were able to stop yourself from repeating the pattern.

_____

_____

_____

_____

_____

_____

_____

_____

_____

_____

_____

Action Step 12 –

Who do you want to be?

In this Action Step you are going to decide exactly what you want from life. You are going to define *your* success. Do these activities:

1. Who do you want to be?

_____

_____

_____

2. Who do you want to be to your family/friends?

_____

_____

_____

3. Who do you want to be professionally?

_____

_____

_____

4. Who do you want to be to yourself?

_____

_____

_____

5. Who do you want to be to God?

_____

_____

_____

6. What do you to achieve financially?

_____

_____

_____

7. What do you want to achieve for your health?

_____

_____

_____

8. What are your thoughts, ideas and feelings about who you want to be?

_____

_____

_____

References

[1] Proverbs 21:21 (NIV)

[2] Proverbs 23:4 (NIV)

[3] Philippians 4:12 (NIV)

[4] to read more about Paul please refer to Acts 8-9 in The Bible:

[5] Dale Carnegie (writer, lecturer 1888-1955)

[6] Proverbs 19:20 (NIV)

[7] Psalm 128 (MSG)

[8] Philippians 4:7 (NIV)

[9] Proverbs 20:18 (NIV)

[10] I do not recommend that you change your own brakes unless you completely understand how and have all the appropriate tools.

[11] 1 Thessalonians 5:17 (NIV)

[12] Author Unknown.

www.ingramcontent.com/pod-product-compliance
Lightning Source LLC
Chambersburg PA
CBHW071744020426
42331CB00008B/2162